MW01595526

The Collected Poems
Of Eric Muirhead

1969 - 2012

Novels by the author
Cab Tales
Rindu A Novel of Expatriate Life in Eastern Malaysia
Eden's Abyss

Copyright © 2013 Eric Muirhead

All rights reserved.

ISBN: 1484842111

ISBN-13: 9781484842119

Library of Congress Control Number: 2013908653

CreateSpace Independent Publishing Platform

North Charleston, South Carolina

Acknowledgements

"Discovery," "Closing Time," and "A Reflection on the Paintings of Mark Rothko's Chapel."Custom Edition for San Jacinto College Central of Literature: an *Introduction to Fiction, Poetry, and Drama.* 9th ed. Ed, XJ Kennedy and Dana Gioia. New York: Pearson Longman, 2005. SJC 129-131.

"A Reflection on the Paintings of Mark Rothko's Chapel" and "Closing Time." *Texas In Poetry 2.* Ed Billy Bob Hill. Fort Worth: TCU Press, 2002. 202-3, 214-15.

"Fabrication Yard Blues." *Lean Seed* 2 (Spring 2002): 13.

"Surrender Point Labuan." *Houston PoetryFest Anthology* 1995. Houston: Houston PoetryFest, 1995. 15-16.

"A Reflection on the Paintings in Mark Rothko's Chapel," and "Closing Time." *Texas in Poetry: A 150 Year Anthology.* Ed. Billy Bob Hill. Denton: Cnter for Texas Studies, 1994. 95, 103-104.

"Early Morning—Singapore." *Western Poetry Quarterly* 4.2 (Spring 1977): 7.

"Closing Time." *Travois: An Anthology of Texas Poetry.* Houston: Ed. J. Whitebird and Paul Foreman. Houston: Contemporary Arts Museum, 1976.135.

"A Reflection on the Paintings of Mark Rothko's Chapel" and "Discovery." *The Fountain* 1.2 (1976): 29-31.

"Oh Come with Me, My Dear." *Western Poetry Quarterly* 3.1 (Winter 1976): 12.

"The Ache." *The Lyric* 56.1 (Winter 1976): 10.

Contents

The Ache

Collected Poems Volume 1

Eric Muirhead

PREFACE

To live, yet burn for more?
Then pull the heart's strings
Tight, more tight, my friend:
The heart will ache, will ache
And someday those strings, they'll break—
Until then though
They'll play you song,
Song to make you yearn for life
To long to burn in life—
A brief candle? Ah! My friend,
The sweet smoke when snuffed
And that broken mandolin a heart,
Cracked in the corner,
Will seal a memory of you.
You will have lived.

WHEN

Alone, alone, alone
Captive
The trees give no peace
The grass–is just grass
The sky
Indifferent
As I write
This day
Another day
Waiting

MEDITATION IN A SCOTTISH STORM

I often come here.
This rock
Above a lonely loch,
And Atlantic winds–
Screaming around stone,
Round scattered tree–
Describe this place.
November rages in Wester Ross,
'Tis always so they say.
Today another gale,
The winds hard from sea
Pitching, buffeting me
Where
A bit absurd
(But poised still)
I have come.
To the limit of hope.
To this rock.

Ah how she blows,
My temptress!
And rips the heather withered wet
(But rooted still)
This storm so easily cruel:
Over the water's dark
Fluries of ghostly forms are fleeing
With the winds

East to dark mouths
Gaping, then closing
In the black mist
There
Tumbling up the mountains
Into the deep past.
This place–of ghastly Gaelic names,
Beautiful names
Their sounds melodic, cruel
Sirens' sounds–
Take me if you will,
Enfold me in your wet black
To the song of cruel earth
so sweet, so sweet.
Swallow another ghost that flees
With the winds
And take him to your dark belly.
There peace?

This the limit of hope.
I have reached the silly end.
November rages in Wester Ross,
'Tis always so they say.

I once cast my lot with men,
With women more,
Busied myself
With the handshake,

With woman's body more.
Sought within a face,
Within the bosom's bed,
In the deep eye
Magic and wonder
And the journey's end.
(I had read of it, you know,
I had heard of it.)
But passion would not rest
Until the end reached here,
Until the dream ended
Here.
On this rock
Above a lonely loch.

Today another gale,
And beneath me
The dark waters are restless,
Where ghostly furies do their dance
Then flee, flee away.

BLACK TENEMENTS

Black tenements sway over the road
And leer their dark innocence at me.
Eyes that look away from empty corners
Concealed within:

> From single dusty rooms

> > Forever passing moons

> > > Forgotten foolish swoons

To turn their gaze on me.

Empty eyes,
they stare at me–
The corpse of a history
That haunts no one.
Do you beckon me enter and take abode?
To sit and muse on a cracked commode?
To feel my hands along ragged walls
Or sip old wine that sickens and palls?
Or would you simply have me die?

Why?

The wind delights along the corners
And screams its pleasure on the night,
As it leaps the road
And races for the mountains,
There to await me further.

GHOSTS

The voiceless ghosts of thoughts that died
Have found a place where they abide.
Their echoes creep upon the wall
Like insect legs confined to crawl,
Whence tingles on the tortured air
A thousand sighs like needles bare,
A fury wrought to painful swell–
Though silent always is my cell.

To the memory of Charles Ives:

RIVER-SOUL AND WIND-SONG

Somewhere far away,
Where misted sleep of winter
Swaddles the plain as ice the little twig,
And bound is planet's flesh
By rib of root and rock:
She pushes her course,
Of ages her course,
Hard upon the torpid muds
Which churly obeisance give
To the dark fever of her destiny.

The sky there is bent upon the land taut
Like a great steel bow,
Its tension glints in the grey silence;
And the wind issues crackling from
The crystalline dew of the prairie grasses
To stalk the brambled banks and brood–
Gazing long upon those swarthy deeps beneath,
Where that forever restless river-soul
Burns black a swath through this fallen world
In urgent keep of her fated way.

Somewhere far away it is,
Where gathering rime lays grip upon the years,
And even death itself lies fallen,
Stuck frozen-clung to the ragged ice:
A river labors through the land
Melting the silence unto a murmur–
A chorus that whispers over the waste
Soft threnode to the ache of life
Throbbing in her virgin bosom,
Where roil the waters to the purpose pent within.

An ancient anguish this
That writhes upon the muds and marl:
The wrath of an innocence
Born to monstrous urge
And the desperate joy that is Alone.
Yet seized by old and chronic sorrows
To see again the swirly river face,
The wind laments in fretted song,
Gives a low moan and then goes crawling,
Almost weeping through the weeds.

LAST NIGHT

I crawled to rest last night
A petty soul,
And thought the vacuous flesh
Did crumble noisily near sleep,
Like sperm-laden urine crepitates
In the deep recess of a toilet bowl.

TO AWAKE. . .

To awake upon the earth of early sunshine
In a place where streets are, concrete
Brick and steel hard wrought and
Bent about, and people rushing
By to clicks that snap from lights that flicker
Red, green, red, green, flushing traffic
Down one pipe and then another
Midst the shimmering roar of heat in writhing
Layers of hot-bellied vapours pressing
Hard to smother those unheeded screams of a baby
Somewhere lost within the walls that lock the spaces–

To awake, I say, upon the earth of early sunshine

LADY

Silent the grief that swells within the sea
This night;
No voice her own to seize the sorrow
And win her free,
This woman giant,
The sea.

Ah! The tired lady,
Bound to the watch of the world's keep:
To cleanse forever the sin and rot
Of man,
And swallow forever the oozing refuse
Of man,
Deep within an anguished belly
That knows no voice.
To bare once more her ancient dugs
At command,
When contemplative men would suckle again
The pure milk of her primitive innocence
Dry,
And leave her pain to pronounce their joy,
Stepping the boot of freedom through the land–
The glory of words, their words–
While exhausted she grips the empty sand.

No voice the grief this night;
Heaves of a silent weariness
That longs for sleep, for sleep.

Ah! My tired lady.

THE ACHE

The ache took root not long ago,
And I an innocent laughing boy
Until those eyes cracked wide my laugh,
And sorrow roared from deep beneath.
O let me kiss those eyes, my dear.
O let me kiss those eyes.

Some seed of yearning rooted there,
And grew a lonely lovely tree.
It blossoms just for you, my dear,
And drops its flowers just for you.
O let me kiss those eyes, my dear.
O let me kiss those eyes.

To bear a flower hurts, my dear;
To lose a flower hurts the more.
Upon the edge of this abyss
I stretch and yearn, yet rooted firm.
O let me kiss those eyes, my dear.
O let me kiss those eyes.

And drop my blossoms to the sea–
That giant maw of woman's heart,
That ancient lust of woman's heart–
My every blossom to the sea.
O let me kiss those eyes, my dear.
O let me kiss those eyes.

To dance again I give no thought,
To sing of grass and boyish flesh,
Because those eyes cracked wide my laugh,
Then wrought my soul unto a tree.
O let me kiss those eyes, my dear.
O let me kiss those eyes.

FANTASIA

Silence steeps in the brimming bosom
Of twilight lolling on the loch:
The earth's pure presence ripens on the air,
Pressing its burgeoning urge upon the parting day
Like the pulp that protrudes through the splitting rind;
While the jaded senses peel away before the breeze,
And the wind-teased flesh leaps
To the pleasure of the cold–
Leaps and would swoon
Upon the water's dark-eyed face,
That mistress I would rape to her deep content,
When the moon rolls full up
From behind the darkling braes,
And settles to his watch like a lily on the land.

LINES COMPOSED ONE SORDID CITY DAWN

The sun is slinking through the murk,
It dawns another day to lurk,
Another day to stare and sigh,
A hot bewildered heathen eye;
For where it once its way could find,
As others of its celestial kind,
Where once it sought the airy steep
Without a thought to laugh or weep:
Now chars its path the churly morn,
Where black miasmal mists are borne,
Now clings like tar the tarnished skies,
Where clam'rous cries on high arise,
And aches that awful globe too oft
To find its way each day aloft;
And struggles more and more to climb
Through this the earth's decay of time,
When broils the blood of men insane,
The bleating voice of heart and vein.

The death is nigh upon us all,
The flames will fly from out he ball
And scream in one torrential burn–
But I to weary sleep return.

AND I FLY

I suffer you see
From less scholarly sludge in the veins.
Where others ponder over book
(And secretly count their woes),
Heavy heads,
I dance
I dance
The pages I lift
In a twirl of toes
And I fly with what I learn in books.

WHISPERS

Wan whispers woo,

Through lakes of moonlit leaves they sough.

Soft cedar breath,

It breathes the quiet call of death–

And life once known,

When she the shifting glades would roam;

Of joy once known,

When she my many dreams did own.

Her moonlit breast

The wanton fires of love caressed;

Her moonlit breast

Fed life to me, to me gave rest.

Where did she go?

The whisp'ring cedars only know.

BLIND

Like the rock on the high mountain
Am I
Unable to see
Blind to the very bone of me

And I can't die

Like the rock of the high mountain
I can't see
This beauty surrounding me
And I'm cold

And I'm old

Like the rock of the high mountain
Mine is a hard pride

THE PHILOSOPHER

The philosopher,
I saw him muttering there,
Muttering old man,
And said, "Sir, please Sir,
What is it that you say?"
He turned and looked,
"I say," he said, "I say there—
I like to go around
Knocking on things, yes,
To see if they are real.
But," he said further, "But sometimes
I like to take a hammer."
He turned, muttering again,
And I, feeling marvelous on the sudden,
Plucking young man,
Went on my way.

I SAW MY MOTHER CRY

I saw my mother cry
Oh God
The pain I saw
Something I had done
Something
Oh God
The pain I saw

OH LISA, LISA!

Oh Lisa, Lisa!
At long last it's happened,
The heart is hollowed now.
The decay of day, alas,
Has come at last to pass. Selah.

Lisa, are you listening?

I need to speak, that is all,
For I am tired, Lisa, so tired,
And fear these moments may elude–
They are harder to hold, Lisa, harder–
And leave me here without a thought,
Without a thought, without a trace,
Without a mask to form my face.
Yes, a mask, my flesh and blood.
'Twas all I ever had, could ever need to have,
For after all, after all, Lisa,
Words are the cream of our creation,
As I have told you many times
Though you never seemed to listen:
The cream I sucked for very life,
While you abstained, always abstained,
And fed your secret wealth some other way
–How, I wonder, how?–
So now you *must* listen, you must,
For I am feeling more and more
The pain and thrill of it decease,
And I must gather it, Lisa,
Hold it to me to the last,
Or else, or else. . .

Lisa, I love you.
But are you there? Are you there?

It's so alone in here, Lisa.
(Are you there? Are you there?)
So still, so deathly still
The caverns of this endless dark.
It freezes on the soul like hoar,
Like hoar it creeps in here,
This silence of a hollowed heart.
I must try to be poetic, you see.
What else now can I be?
And words are the cream of creation,
As I have told you many. . .
Or so I said already, so I said.

But Lisa, can you hear me?
Can you hear?

The silence seems to swallow up
My every word, my every sound,
This black, black silence of a hollowed heart.
It's tongued out my very sight, Lisa.
Like some ageless vulture come, it devours
This poor pâté of time and space
I once conceived as soul. Hah!
Do you hear, Lisa? The soul.
A mighty word once, to me.
Though you laughed to hear me speak it.
How you laughed to hear me speak it.
Will you laugh now?
Please laugh now.

Yet don't you hear me?
Don't you hear?

I would only speak the truth, Lisa,
But something, I fear, is fouling me.
The truth, the simple truth, you see,
For words are all there are, to me.
And words are the cream of crea. . .

Am I silly? Am I sad?
Am I frightened to be mad?

The flesh, Lisa, it too is gone.
Rotted away it did, rotted.
Then who am I, or what?
I feel nothing in here, Lisa.
Can you imagine nothing?
And yet it is something, but what?
Something unseen, unheard,
Unknown, and it crawls here, Lisa.
It's something awful in here–

I simply must talk, you see.
(If you hear, if you hear)
This nothing creeps like mold
Its fingery way along the rot.
Hah! I will stab it with words,
Scream into the silence words,
Down the vast corridor of eternal night
Scream, scream, scream!
For nothing will surely hear me.
Hah! A pun, a pun,
A sad, delicious little pun.
(Am I silly? Am I mad?)
Spin words into eternity
And what do you have?
Eternity. Just another word.
And the rest is silence.

Selah. Selah. Selah.

But now 'tis harder, Lisa.
Harder, words are harder. . .
I said I loved you,
Didn't I? . . . didn't I? . . .
Harder, words are harder. . .
And nothing creeps like mold. . .

Words, they're passing now,
Passing away. . . away we go. . .
But a word. . . one word. . .
Remains. . . one word. . . one. . .
Lisa, Lisa. . .
      Lisa. . .
         Lisa

POOR REFLECTIONS

To soar into remote skies
I do adore, I do adore,
For dreams are all there are
Any more. Are all there are
To stave the pain
Of labored breath and heavy brain;
This ache that cramps the eyes,
When while awake I hide the sighs
And feign to please the world–to walk
As those with reason to exist
(Called style and place, appropriate grace),
To talk. Yet would you know it's true,
I but subsist and that's the clue
Behind this mask that binds the face–
Behind these eyes and mouth that smile
(Because I fain would live awhile).
I but subsist, I can but seem,
And dream, and dream. . .

To soar into remote skies
I do adore, I do adore,
For dreams are all there are
Anymore.

A CALL

A wisp of winter air
That woos along the ground,
Where frosted furrows white
With early morning snow
Crack to the leather step
Of city shoes. A call
From deep within a wood,
A sigh that breathes the wind
And shapes a coyish course,
As I still follow on.
Still follow on, and find
A sudden to my side
A tenement of white
Set solid on the snow.
Cut black into the stone
The windows frame a crowd
Of olive children there,
That stare, that stare,
Their mouths in wide despair.
And then the call again
From deep within a wood.
I follow on.

DELIVERANCE

Hot sun
Soaking in the mist
Of noon-day.
Flesh that shivers
to the sweat of panic
Seeping on the scene.;
Hot sun,
Freeing the pores
Of a skin
Closed against the world,
And afraid, afraid.
Hot sun,
Delivering the soul
Now running from its bonds,
Its easy bonds,
Running to the ground
To die, to die
Sucked by the thirsty dirt.
Hot sun
soaking in the mist
Of noon-day,
You're killing me,
You're killing me.

HOUSTON SCENARIO

PREFACE

A feeling, grown rich on the
fat of time's labor, meets
suddenly the unknowable, grows
uncertain, brittle–then disintegrates
in shards, revealing
the bare core: a breath, hesitant,
but now young and eager
to breathe.

I

Another hot day dissolves into dusk;
The cool rolls to the ramble of a breeze,
And blue, blue the bleached skies deepen to dark.
The blistered sun gropes beyond bayou trees;
Enmeshed in leaves and tumid, itchy mists,
Tangled in vine, gropes, and stumbles away
To plains and worlds beyond. But, before gone,
Turns, and magnanimous fellow he is,
Gleams a smile that lasts a while, and glows warm
On the big clouds that scramble like fleshy boys
For a last glimpse: ruddy cheeks and buttocks
Of clouds sprawled upon the gloam for a glimpse.

"Ah, Mother Nature,
Your breast is vast and nipple sweet!
God bless that big sun you bore in high heat,
And all the boys and girls that grapple for your teat!"

The city steel and stone instead, raise high
A solemn head, towers of grey and white,
Which grave of mien into the peeling light
Erect; though yet can't reach those parting thighs
Of quivering curves of cloud alive
(Which now like mythic maids do writhe!).

But the steel and the stone remain, they stay,
While all those wonders now wander away.
> For it is time now.
They stay, and up into a sobered sky do pile
Hulking shells of hope against another night's trial.
> For it is time now.
> It is time.

II

A city in soul stirs slow in the night.
Slow the limbs to feel the veins open, gape,
Hungry for the suck.
The taut fibers of a day's long bother loosen,
And the rank smell of feet and pouring sweat
Lifts from the hot walks to cool the tired air,
To cool and to rouse,
Prodding, prodding a city's soul to stir
And walk the rich night, drink of the rich night.

A city in soul stirs slow in the night.

For something seeps into a city's soul
As darkness stretches and draws toward dreams:
The visions of those bastard joys which drip
From memory's lonely, forlorn cell, the gleams
That are the moonlight on a city's soul.
And in the grey air of the half-cast light
Is a madness born, is a hunger born
For the suck of rank flesh a-sweat in the night,
Of creaturely love alive in the night,
Of love, of love, and alive in the night.

SIR WIND

Ah! The wind
Kiss Kiss Kiss
Has come again.
Cool fingers in the hair,
Probing gently now,
Kiss Kiss Kiss
Probing freely now,
Tingling in the loins,
Ah! Maddening in the loins
Feeling, feeling, cool fingers
Unashamed.
Kiss Kiss Kiss
Would you love me, wind?
Would you love me?
Like the full leaves
Ripened to gold,
To the full splendor,
Aching for your touch,
For your gentle, incessant touch?
Tugging now, yes tugging.
Ah! Sir wind
Would you love me?
Kiss Kiss Kiss
Madden this full flesh
To tears that drip, drip
Into your gath'ring embrace?
That wet your arms, your face,
And sparkle so
On your cool, cool fingertips?
Oh! Darling wind,
Would you love me?
Tear me like the leaf
and bear me?
Kiss Kiss Kiss
    Said the wind, said the wind.

TWO BIRDS

Two birds are flying over the red Gargantuan plain.

One dipping, turning, twirling, the other bearing straight,

But both together in flight, as 'twere mates, or comrades,

Together flying westward over the red Gargantuan plain.

One dipping, tossing in the earth-red air, doing spins;

The other, wings wide and pumping, aiming straight,

The ruddy sun brilliant in the fixed eyes.

Two birds, big and black against the sun, flying together

Over the flesh-red plain, the stone silence

Of eons beaten to bitter red clay, the stone silence

Of this the last, last plain, where two birds are flying,
    westward,

One doing spins and twirls, the other bearing straight,

But both together in flight, as 'twere mates or comrades,

Together flying westward over the red Gargantuan plain.

A WOMAN'S NAME

I can hear it rapping on the glass
    (Gentle, gentle on the glass)
I can hear it stepping through the grass
    (Softly, softly through the grass)
I whirl 'round
And there it wets my face,
Laughing, laughing wets my face;
Then away upon the wind somewhere,
Away upon the wind,
A wild, delicious laugh somewhere
Away upon the wind.
I hear it there, I hear it,
Melting into meadows, into far places,
A summer rain in far places,
Somewhere stepping through the grass
    (Like warm rain wept)
Somewhere rapping on the glass;
Somewhere laughing,
Somewhere crying–I hear it
Somewhere dying:
A woman's name,
A woman's name.

THE NIGHT IT HOWLED

It was like the original Adam
In each one of us
Screaming for revenge
In each one of us
That night the howl leapt
And danced to the sky
Mad, mad it was
Out there, in the sky
And all around the crushing weight
Of it, rising in some bizarre crescendo
In each one of us I tell you
The moon, too, took up the yell
In full-faced glory yelled
And the city shook
To the ground shook, then crumbled
Under those shock waves of yell
Ripping all asunder
In each one of us
To grains of atom
Settling like a white smoke
Over all, as quiet came
And the moon appeared to smile
Yes, I believe it smiled
And Adam rose then
From the rubble rose
Shook his shoulders of the dust
Then strode off, laughing
To where the sun would rise
Laughing

REMEMBERING

Her face was there and soft,
Like the moon soft in mist of warm seas
There in the night her face.
There to touch (but I could not),
There to kiss (but I could not),
There to love, to love?
But I could not.

So dies the moment.

MONOLOGUE

Midday
The stillness drifting heavy on this arena
Like an exhausted lover

The sea falling back
Sky writing with trembling moves
Of clouds, big, steamy clouds

Boiling as if to burst the chains
Of some protracted, unbeaten bondage
But hushed, silenced in their torment

The sea falling back
Like an exhausted lover
falling back

Melancholy
With no words to call upon
No words to call upon

It Is Rain in the Mountains

Mountains

Collected Poems Volume 2

—❀❀❀—

By
Eric Muirhead

IT IS RAIN IN THE MOUNTAINS

It is rain in the mountains
Weep rocks
Weep with me
Exuberance of catharsis
Rent from heaving sky
On bare stone caught
Wild like a bird
Screaming for wings
"Weep rock!"
And the bird afire and furious
Streams 'cross rain-pommeled chasms
Her burst and bleeding love:
Renders birth upon the storm
"Weep rock!
Weep with me!"

It is rain in the mountains
A madness crying
"Weep, weep with me"
Dying into rain and emptiness
Coursing cut stone and breast wet
With tears wept
Raining, yes raining
Down far down to soft earth
Deep into cleft
But healed places of the valley's soft
Caressed depth
Where life grows, is fruitful
And womanhood delights
In sunshine of after-rain
Glowing on new-born cheeks.

THE WANDERER'S QUESTION AND THE MOCKINGBIRD'S REPLY

1. DO YOU KNOW?

Do you know
When you've come the long way
And conceive at last
For life there is no answer
Because no question's there
(But only here, only here
Where mind plots dread and fear)
Do you know
When you've climbed and seen
Life at last from the hilltop
In the clear clean light of day
At last at last from the hilltop
Where mind does not hld sway
(Though poor thoughts still peep at life,
Peep and laugh, peep and laugh)
Do you know
How tired at the hilltop
The mind would have us be
When once we've seen life free?
How heavy, dull, monotonous
The mind would have life be
Once seen from the hilltop, seen free?
Do you know
Do you know
The hatred for one
Who's come the long way
And seen the innocence there
Where life no longer cares
What mind prescribes?
Do you know
The fatigue at the hilltop
Mind heart-sick now life at last is free?

Do you know
Do you know
How mind can drown us in disgust
At the sight of ourselves free?

2. REPLY

I know I know I know

The mockingbird then said

So listen so listen so listen

To my joyous melody

To my joyous melody

A TOAST

I know not where
I know not when
It will come on me:
A feverish delight
At the sight of these
Creatures of our kind
All about. Main Street,
Shoreline, all night cafè, or
Where art where fashion
Summon the eye,
Faces, bodies–lively,
Sad, poor or lavish,
Or lean, lean, lean–
Move and make life be.
Is it sad, is it stupid
What I see about me,
Silly perhaps?
Is it ugly?
Is it beauty?
Is it love or disgust?
What matter, I say.
It is life, it lives
Because it must, it must.
Will you not cheer
That the show goes on,
Exclaim with me, "Hurray?"

BAYOU

Bayou
Slow moving water-king
Of green earth's shallows,
Soggy flats of land's end
Sinking toward sea.
Water of the ancient earth
This slow stream of the land,
Seepage
From the mud and wet life,
The sodden deeps of an old earth
Still nursed by the sea,
Rooted
Deep in the silences of the sea:
Hushed
But for water
Moving through time
Slow through time
As bayou eases toward sea.

Life is rich here,
Rich in its own slow urge
To broaden, imbibe the heat's heavy damp,
Mature into rank quiet
And riot of life profuse as still.
Then die again into water,
Into bayou
Moving toward sea,
Slow through this early world,
Quiet stealth of the water-king
Easing his way with a dignity
Toward sea, toward sea.

Beside the Buffalo Bayou
Houston, 1975

LABIE

I am the soul of Labie.
I've wandered the world's ends,
Harbored pity, known shame
As I, stumbling lame,
Have witnessed the centuries pass.
Born in a desert waste
Was I, far away
From the lands men know
A long, long time ago—
suckled milk of human paps
In that wild place,
The tender, timid paps
Of a mere girl.
In a cave in the high rock
Alone we lived
Far above the yellow plain:

> *With the plant, the deer*
> *And the wild cat,*
> *She and I.*

It had happened, she said,
She had fled a slave train
Long en route from her land,
Had wandered, and when about to die,
He came to her, he,
A figure risen from the winds

And the wild rock,
Labie (she whispered his name
When nights were dark and cold),
He came and took her and loved her
As his child. A creature
Of keen eye and lean
She said, though old now:

>   *Like human, like cat,*
>   *Like the deer of the high rock,*
>   *Though old now.*

He made a home for her, found food,
Both meat and the plant they ate;
Then nights he wooed her eyes to his.
Quiet attended their flame-lit room,
While far away, from somewhere,
Terror howled and moaned,
Faintly from somewhere far
Beyond light of the full moon
When the plain shown a silent silver sea,
And quiet attended the high rock.
Then it was, she said to me,
There came a night with winter near
When Labie held her, enfolded her.
In me his soul rooted the hour
She conceived. It was a night
Of witchy winds she'd say,
And they tossed in their love upon gypsy dreams

And she screamed through the night
To the pleasure of wild body's love.
Morning he was dead beside her,
The man like human, like cat,
Was no more but the limp creature of a corpse
Left behind when his soul left.

> *Quiet came again.*
> *Deep quiet,*
> *Her belly ripe with child.*

From our lair we watched the snows,
We watched the sands,
Seasons turned.
What did I see?
I saw her, once young, a girl,
Now growing old–
The work of life wore her,
Her dugs were limp
When I was still a lad.
But it was not sad with us:
Her skin against my cheek,
The cool cave rock beneath my feet,
The dry air of the desert noon
And the moon upon our bed–
It was not sad with us.
We knew love
Natural as the eye's glance
She and I, as a dream in sleep,
Love deep with the quiet of our world.

She was old, she died.

I buried her and left.

A pity was hid there

In the heart of the love we knew:

> *But not from fear,*
>
> *Not from shame.*
>
> *From innocence alone it grew.*

I am lame.

Across the wide plain

A boar became my foe.

I watched it writhe in the pain of my grasp,

Fear was there in the screaming eye.

I tended by leg and limped

Into the world of man.

> *And I saw:*
>
> *Fear was there,*
>
> *Deep in the screaming eye.*

So I've watched, so I've listened.

The son and soul of the man

Like human, like cat,

Like the deer of the high rock,

I've wandered, and I've learned

How men make words, make tools

To beat the innocence back

Deep in the quiet I know.

Their noise, their cries

Their whispers

Deafen and confuse.

I have felt the sting of scorn–shame.

How helpless is the heart of man

That the pity deep in the heart of love

Is gone;

That piety, duty, and fear

Burrow there and chatter,

Noisy and loathesome creatures

Waving little swords;

That words of men crawl

Like insects on a lovely plant

Eating the precious leaves,

And hate and shame are left

Like the stump.

> *How helpless is the heart of man:*
> *His love must always be his*
> *Fear of life, his fear of death.*

I must back to the quiet

Of the high rock,

Back across the plain to the wild waste

Where words (she whispered, "Labie,"

When nights were dark and cold)

Are like the moon of a dry night

Falling soft on the bed of her

And the boy by her breast.

Where fierce shrill of the winds,

Soft silence of the stars

And the image of her

Calling me, calling me,

All speak of a pity

Deep in the heart of love,

A quiet, a quiet

That is the one innocence.

> *Where Labie goes now,*
> *For he is old*
> *And he must.*

PASSION DRY

Passion
Dry as prairie grass
Stalk-life
Cracking into dust

Dry, spent
Broken from stalk

Ragged thing blistered
Passion
Dry
Dust
Death

I crave water!

THE POET AND THE CRITIC

"The heart, the *heart*," the poet cried,
"That's where to look for verse to write."
"No, no," the critic sighed.
"That's trite, that's trite.
Look for something new to write."

"The mind then, *mind*," the poet claimed.
"There's matter there for verse to write."
"No, no!" the critic blamed,
"That too is trite.
Look for something new to write."

"Ah, sex then, *sex*!" the poet leered.
"The subject's ripe and always right."
"No, no!" the critic reared
"That's trite, that's trite.
Look for something new to write."

The poet looked confused,
The critic unbemused.
"What can I do?" the poet wept.
"I do not know!" the critic leapt.
"But just be sure that it is new!"

LINES

A sadness beyond time
Is on me.
It won't change
With the clock.
Everywhere I see life
Even in the unliving
The rock, the sand
The rainwater of our earth—
Life, with no reason to be
Dumb
With no tongue that speaks.
A man or a woman speak
(A bird sings)
They hear themselves,
Are heard.
But what makes them be
Man, woman, or bird
It has no tongue
Is dumb
Deep in all that is
Even in the unliving.
Tongues only mimic stones.

END

In Four Short Pieces

That it's happening
Cannot be denied:
Night has walked onto the prairie
For the last time.
The world has its eyes to the prairie,
For it is the very last time.
The sun, they say, will never rise again.

On the prairie the telephone poles
Parade before the last light,
Gaunt last silhouettes
In silent salute.
West the black clouds are closing
On the great red wound in the sky,
The dying sun,
Earth's last blood flowing
Before the gaunt poles and wires–
Testament of life
Once proud, once master.
The clouds have closed.
Tarry night has won the world,
The sun is dead.

A scream is heard.
Across the high flat-lands
Penetrating the dark
A woman's scream.
Then the hoarse-throated slow sigh
Of dumb pain
Gripping its nails
In the silent soil of the night.
For the last time.

Now wanders over the black cold
Unseen
Eyes.
Through the whispers of a raw wind
A beat rises
Ha! Ha!
Dry beat
Coming to chorus
Ha! Ha!
From out of the black of night
The howl
Ha! Ha!
Ha! Ha!
Loud
Everywhere
Ha! Ha!
Ha! Ha!
Ha! Ha!
Rising to the wind's raw throat
Everywhere

ANNOYED

Chatter
Like incessant spilling of wine
On the clean white table-cloth
Newly washed and waiting
For the diners of an elegant mode and speech.
Chatter
People spilling
Everywhere staining
The white of quiet
Spread for the dinner
And the wine that awaits
The diners
Who know speech
Is the art of taste and a fine palate
And do not foul the table
By always spilling, staining.

SCENE

The sky is rolling
Wind alive
Cloud black

A road
Two pounded ruts
Where wheels have beat
The caked grit of the plain
A gulch
Mesquite trees crowding it
Waiting for water
(When it comes)
Watching for water

Rain at last

A man
Old
Sits by the road
Above the gulch
Sits
Skin long beaten by sun
And dust of this place
Waits
Face to the sky

The sky is rolling
Burdened is rolling

Eyes
Old
Trained to sun's lash

And the dust of this place
Squinting to the sky
Hollows of sight

Beat from his face
They wait
They watch

The sky is rolling
Wind alive
Cloud black

A road
A gulch
A man old
Eyes old
Mesquite
All beat
Out of caked grit of the plain
Waiting for water
(When it comes)

The sky is rolling
Burdened is rolling
Rain at last

ON THE STEPS AGAIN

The sun arose
As usual
in this hot time of year
Through the wet smoky east
Of bay water, sea air
And hot factory pipes.
A woman walked
Reviewed her flowers
Tended her dreams.

City streets yawned
As usual
With drone of the engines
The cars crowding the day
With their kind of life.
Caseous breath of old lungs
The city breathed again
When the sun at noon-day
Stood stock still.

All today
As usual.
Stock still
As usual.
A woman with kerchief in hand
Wipes her brow
And waters
As she again reviews her flowers
Tends her dreams.

JUST DUST

Shadows dim the room.
Clouds
Slow emotionless
Creatures, these that pass
Dimming precious sun.
Rain
Must it come again
Flat unresonant
Patter, endless days.

Blues
Hopes long nurtured here
Dead non-functioning
Remnants, they're just dust.

FUGUE AND DREAM

Through a window
Open on the night rain
A fugue:
Trained fingers
Shaping a dream
Off piano keys
Urging it to birth.
A life's sadness
Stepping from the parlour
Through the window
Into the raining night.

The rain continues
Night closes deeper
The player works on.
Then slipping through the leaves
And wet drip of rain
I see
In white wet gown
His song:
A maiden there stepping 'cross the grass
Her smile
Crossed by the many tears of rain.

SCENARIO

The cry went high
"Rejoice!"
High into the sparkling sky
And galloped far
To distant corners of the town,
Where the prairie lay golden
This morn, lay golden.

*

What was it started that?
Busy bathing in my tub
Washing away the soul's dirt
I found vexatious
This endless "Rejoice!"
Jumping like a bean all over town.
I heard the people gather down below:
"*Rejoice! Rejoice!*
Now isn't it a beautiful day?"
'No! I splashed
And slapped more soap on,
"And it a working day, too!"
(The bath was filthy,
I would have to drain it
And fill it still again.)

"Rejoice! Rejoice!"
I looked outside, irked:
The whole town was there,
Kissing, hugging in the streets,
And it a working day, too!
What was it started that?
Enough! I jumped in a fresh bath
(Damn! It again turned mud)
Splashed and slapped soap on

*

"Rejoice!" they cried.
"Damn!" he sighed.
Your choice, I say–
Ah! But the prairie lay golden
This morn, lay golden.

DISCOVERY

Last night (near death)
Slumped on concrete
Beside some street
Where love at last
Abandoned me
In distaste fled
I lay me down
Upon the street
To gaze, quiet
Into the sky.
The city slept
Deep in dank wet
Of its own sweat
But barely stirred.
The buildings rose
Aloof and proud
Big tall keepers
Of the great hopes
And dreams, the plans
Of other men
Than me, they rose
Ignoring me
And kept their watch
By night. Alone
At last alone
Cast out and left
Where love had fled
And pity too
Beyond desire
I lay me down
Last night to die
Flat on that street

Gazing, quiet
Into the sky.

But strange to say
Something sufficed:
I saw the sky
Quiet, and deep
Beyond all life
Adrift, the sky
Silent in night
Beyond all dreams
(The towers kept
For those that slept)
Adrift, and deep
Flat on that street
Gazing, quiet–
The sky, I saw
The sky.
What pride was mine
Beyond all love
Alone last night
What pride was mine
Beyond all life
Adrift (near death)
Last night. I lived.

A WARNING

Junk gathers,
Cities grow big with it.
Piles of it
Clog the metropolis.
The streets, cars
People pushing for space
All strain, strain
To move junk and clear room,
But junk clogs;
The cities' old bowels
Can't move it.

It's boredom
Sits and eats junk, spits junk
And groaning
Shits it too.–Boredom's come
To millions
Of American tired
Affluent
We've lost the dream, the drive
To be free,
And just sit, boredom's come.
Will death too?

July, 1975

SEDUCTION
(DELIVERANCE, A SEQUEL)

The brain sleeps,
Fatigued–
Or was it bored?–
Sleeps now.
The legs move
Arms they respond.
Belly still aches:
Craves food
Or hates, rejects it
In disgust–
But brain sleeps.
The summer sun
Dreaming on the vines,
The cicada hum
And drip of catalpa sap
Have coaxed it away,
Into the rich green
And dank, pungent earth
Have coaxed it
So easily away.
This body asks
Who, what is it?
The legs move,
Arms
They respond.
And belly always aches,
But the principle's gone.
So who, what is this
Trying to think now,
Trying. . .

I should wish for cold tundra,
A mountain's awesome height,
Northern seas ripping

Heave upon heave of white wave:
But
Southern summer
Hot, still,
The sweat of the body's
Just subsisting
Just *e*-xisting;
Hum and drip of life primitive,
No longer thinking,
Just flesh
Freed
Delivered of its principle,
Hot, and hungry
Without reason
(Belly aching, always aching,
But without reason)–
Just flesh freed.
Southern summer
It claims me again
(Was I fatigued?
Or just bored, perhaps);
Seduced
I am delivered again,
Living animal again.

HARRY TALKS ABOUT WINNING,
AT A BAR WITH SAM

Why this game of winning
Should count so
I don't know,
But it does count, Sam.
Ooo, the blood
Demands it;
Winning,
The triumph.
Not saying, "I'm the best,"
But winning, silently,
Instinctively,
In command of the moment
To retire with merely a bow.
Ah, that's it, Sam:
With merely a bow.

How can you live
And not ask, "*How good*
Am I?"
How good are you, Sam?

We love to judge.
What would we be
If we didn't
Love to judge?
We wouldn't be.

It's our stuffing, our reason.
Whoever thought love was not
Judging,
Judging,
And liking what one sees?
Yes, man can't love
But to win, Sam,
Or love one who does.
Yet don't forget:
It's not saying, "I'm the best,"
But just winning, silently,
Instinctively,
In command of the moment
To retire with merely a bow.
Ah, that's it!
Sam, whadoya say?

WEALTH AND DEATH

Do you believe
There's future here?
Ugliness spreads,
Man can't design around it,
Can't.
Cities are crowded
With affluence:
Wealth has become
Its own teeming garbage,
A fruitful cancer
It blocks the way,
Wherever impulse choose to go
It blocks the way.
Anger.

Wealth.
It's America's anger now,
Her peace no more
Prosperity no more.
I see she's confused, poor girl:
She calls for more wealth–
Bring it! Bring it!–
More
To beautify the ugly
That grows on the face
Of our land;
The cosmetics of wealth

She applies, confused–
Poor girl,
She's old
And the dreams that were once
Are her nightmare now;
For ugliness spreads,
We can't design around it
Or master the anger either,
The disappointment
That we may have reached an end.
Is a new birth still possible?
Can America conceive again?
Is there a future here,
I ask, I ask?

IN WONDERMENT OF THE MOON ONE NIGHT

The moon follows its course
Around earth
The earth follows its course
Around sun
The sun follows its course
Through the galaxy.
Through the galaxy
Order and pattern
Infinite
Impersonal
Perfect.
All bodies
Perfect
And in place
Through space
Through space.

And man sits
Atop a midden
Watching.

THE FALL

Seeking the profound vision
He often stumbled,
Fell in pits.
He wouldn't cry,
No that wasn't his way,
Or curse,
But would lie there
Where he had fallen,
Learning to listen
To what life lived there
In the pits
The holes
The bogs
He encountered
When he fell.
He learned
As he lay there
(Soiled but discreet)
Life could be heard
When not seen.
When not seen profoundly
It could be heard profoundly:
It was not quite a beat,
Not quite a sigh,
Not a whisper
Or a cry,
And he despaired sometimes
Trying to say to himself
What it was he heard.
It was–*a flow*
Running
Through the rock
Through the soil
Through the trees, he heard it
Running
A flow of deep
Caressing power:

The earth's veins
Alive, deep, full
And bounding with tensions
That loved to leap and dive,
To flow on and on–
Perpetual orgasm
Deep in the earth's belly.
He heard it.

All this he learned
To hear
When he stumbled
And he fell
Headlong into the pits
He often failed to see,
And would lie awhile
Where he was fallen
Listening.
But seeking the profound vision
He couldn't rest,
But grew impatient,
Arose from the fall
To push on,
His eyes
Again rooted to the sky,
His ears
Again listening to his words,
His spirit–
Visionary again.

PARTING

It was in late November
Cold rain in the city
Twinkled in the cold
Glimmering light of a streetlamp
Alone (grey, grim
Marker to eternity)
Near a dark corner
Where two dark lovers stood
She
I
Staring
With stoic faces
(The cry was over now)
But not quite into one another's eyes.
Just missing
Seeing instead the dark
Beyond
Of nothing now
Haunting the rim of a long, long night
To be somehow endured now.
No tears
(There was the rain)
Fears only
And the terrible, terrible
Disappointment in two stoic faces.
It had failed.
She turned and walked from me
Gathered in grey coat
Hands tucked in the pockets deep
She walked from me.
Painfully her form
Entered the streetlamp's shower

Of glimmering, cold tears
Dripping in the grey, grim light
Then disappeared into nothing.
It had failed.

I would stand a while
There
A long while in a cold rain
Trying to measure the significance.
But all I saw
Was her hair, dark hair
As it sparkled
Painfully
When she crossed beneath
The cold lonely streetlamp
(Last marker to eternity)
And disappeared into nothing.

FOR A MAN NAMED SHOSTAKOVITCH

A hot Texas night
A fan whirred in the gloom
It was quiet abroad
The air lay heavy as it was hot.
But I brought to life a music
In my room that night
A passacaglia, creation
Of a man far away
A Russian whose soul
Played strings for me
Dire, passionate
Broody strings for me
Eloping into utmost beauty on the night—
Essence of pain of joy
Bitter, bittersweet
But fragrant, so fragrant on the night.
The music called
I had stepped through the hot gloom
And entered the cold, dark night
Of Russian pathos, old
So old it takes the earth
Into its hands
Nurtures the darkest instincts
Into life again, nurtures
The greatest love into life again
Blossoming
And tendering even a hot Texas night

Far away
The attar of its pure
Cold exhilarating fire
The passion
Of a people long in pain
And a man, their musician.

CONTEMPLATION ON THE DECEASE OF A LOVE ZEAL

How many ways to waste a day.

Waste?
What is waste?

Vast plain of time
Shimmering in nude sun–
Time fallen from flight
To sand, burnished
Beat to deadness
To sand–
Desert (oneself alone). A rock
Might lie in one direction
An awkward rock
Far away, indifferent
Nothing else to be seen
(Fancy died and time tumbled
Broke to bare sand, indifferent–
Fantasy, it seems
Is only a mirage of life
Lifted on the sands of oneself alone
Walking nowhere).
So you walk
Wondering where in this whole
Ludicrous place to go.

How many ways to waste a day?

How many deserts in an hour

Where time

Is but bare sand underfoot

(The sun nude, indifferent)

Leading where

Beyond all delight and spring of life

All forgetfulness and fancy

Beyond all that is not dead (but loves yet)–

Time is the dour

End that is no end.

A SENSUALIST IN THE ORCHARD

I plucked the lady.
A ripe fruit was she
Begging, begging there
To be eaten.
She had come of age
Her breasts were full
As if the milk already
Wanted to be sucked
And she squirmed
In my hand pleading
With all her body's tensions
To draw my mouth
Down on her. Now,
I thought, observing her,
Is this decent? Yes,
I thought, admiring her,
This is decent.
For I am hungry,
And she
Is hungry. So,
I brought my mouth
Down on her, bit.
Ah! A good taste.
She squealed as the rind
   burst,
My teeth sank
And the wet pulp took.

For Susan:

WISTFUL

I would I were
A mountain bird,
Free to fly
In sky where cliff
And rising rock
Look on the blue–
Vast sea, eternal sea,
Lapping
Their distant, forbidding world
Where always, they are
Monarch.
A mountain bird
Lifting its wings
Above palaces
Where kings are real
(Not forsaken to fairy-tale,
But beauty hard, real
These kings)
Free to fly
Where always, always
There drifts unearthly air
About the thrones
And throne-rooms,–
Giving truth to the old myth
Of God's city in the sky.

PASSAGE

Twilight.
Moonlight weeps
Through wet boughs
That bend, gnarled
Rent of life
To dew beds below,
Where autumn death
Congeals deep into the weave
Of the cold dark ground.
Here
Silence walks first this evening.
In the white robes of the fallen moonlight,
Dew-rippled robes,
Silence walks, and
Sadness hints its presence
In every fold: the tears
The moonlight weeps are there.
Now
Black boughs
Creak in a cold rush
Of sudden wind
From over the hills.
Dead vines crackle,
Dew hardens to specks of ice
Glittering–
Tears no longer drip
But moonlight sticks

To bark and bindweed,
Sticks and seems to laugh now
Low, sinister, rising on the night,
This night:

                        Another passage
In slow, slow time's
Unceasing year of change.

AMERICAN CHILD

She played with the cats
In her parlor she was
Enwrapped with her world
Dark, lean
American child
This woman,
Purring with the cats
She spoke no words
Sitting cross-legged
And pleased,
Eyes dark, wide
And laughter caressing her throat
Rounding her mouth–

I sat
To her parlor come
Talked of struggles
Heartache, passion
I talked of passion
(There was a story in her eyes
I could see it, of the
Profound womanly knowledge
The haunted wants
Desires of unordinary need)
Talked. But
She played with the cats
Purred, giggled into laughter

Running her hands over her small breasts
To brush from her blouse the animal hair
Heard no words I said—

I could see a story
Yet untold
Furtive her eyes gave hint
Basking in the glory of cats
Hint of some dark deep
At the edge of which
I felt my words collapse
Then fall
Lost in a deep silence—
From which, however
Giggles and laughter suddenly rose
In a resounding flood
Of primeval grotesqueness.
I was appalled, and fled
Giggles leaping in my wake
Fled, sought in books, words
To constitute, fashion again
Something of sanity. Fled.

CLOSING TIME

*(On Hempstead Road, headed northwest out of Houston, stands a small motel
in a lonely line of warehouses and freight depots, called AParadise. It is a favor-
ite resting place for roughnecks, cowboys, working men in town for a few days.)*

Just another joint:
Men all stare
Over beer pools in glasses
Scattered and long neck bottles;
A worn but friendly woman serves,
Trying to look a bit sexy
In short red cowhide skirt.
Men stare at dark walls
Merging in a delirium of haze,
A bit of stink, and dreams–
Listen to the juke box
Whimper hurt tones of unrequited
Love for them. Hysteria breeds
In undertones of choked
Hurt. Burning flesh points
Of cigarette mouths
Float drunk in raw smoke.
A woman serves,
Trying to look a bit sexy.

2:00 AM. Time to close.
Law requires.

The lights out.
Juke box
Quiet, unplugged.
Hysteria–contained
In shadows, harmless.
A cowpoke's the last to leave,
Called a taxi;
Slips in beside the driver:
"Paradise, please Sir."

Chant

Collected Poems Volume 3

—∞∞∞—

By
Eric Muirhead

EARLY MORNING–SINGAPORE

Wet:
The mat of island
That dawn sucks
Through the glooms
Of its approach.
No breath.
Palm trees
Stick
In damp sky–
Fronds choke.
Luxuriant weight
Of the stiff leaf
Hangs.
Then hear
Faint pulse
Of dying energy:
'Ihrough the dawn water
Thousands wake.
They walk.
The red rust
Of a thousand roofs
Is their color,
Their blood color.

Day does not emerge
Or arise here;
It is only another shade
Of night the red rust
The wet green
Breed in.

SURRENDER POINT, LABUAN

(A small island off the northwest coast of Borneo, Labuan was the site of a major encounter in June, 1945, between the landing forces of the Australian 9th Division sweeping up from the island's southern beaches, and the 32nd Japanese Southern Army dug into the hills to resist them. The junk of war is still there, strewn through the jungle, the downed planes, the bombed jeeps, a tangled, decaying wreckage giving way to vine and a reflourishing canopy; but the ghosts of the dead are there too, unappeased, if the locals are believed. On Labuan's west beach the remnants of the 32nd at last succumbed to the Australians. It is a place now consecrated to peace, where a dense coconut grove faces the expanse of the South China Sea. The shore here is gradually sinking, forming lagoons littered with the trunks of fallen palms.)

Hysterical

A cock crows
From deep in the coconut grove's
Quiet stature of repose;
Indifference lights the green sea's
    calm,
The white shore a graveyard
Of fallen palms quietly
Worked from roots' hold,
Broken from land,
Returned to origins.

A cock in the grove somewhere,
Hysterical, crows. A coconut
Bursts on the beach. The silent fall
Might have begun years ago.
The sun slants exotically
Through fronds of palm leaves
Warm, cautious
Oriental sun.
The sea eats at the land
Lazy, patient.
A cock

Crows,
Crows.

The long afternoon drifts
Veiling the peace.
A tall palm inclines further,
About to fall, crash to water,
A cock somewhere
The hush of the dead
The many years
The sea eating them
Crows
Deep in the coconut grove, hysterical
Bursts, bleeds.
The slant light of the sun
Timid in the deep there
Greets darkness, screams.

COMPOST

Scraps of a life
All gluey with need
Thrown together
Spread on a warm heart

Flowers sometimes grow there

TWO MOODS

CLOSED

Sitting
Working for a thought
Looking at odds and ends
Dangling my pen
My penis

Whether it's abyss
Or desk top
Or cunt
Sometimes makes no difference–
The matter's closed.

Open Again

"Oh fuck!"
I heard it resound
Through canyons
Startle mountains
The deer scattered

Then morning managed
To absorb the disgrace.
The ripe sun whistled
The deer gathered again.
It was all in the family.

NUDE GIRL

Nude girl
On the beach
Looks seaward.
Mountains rise
Beyond stretch of sea: blue
Nude nature, arms open.
Something hurts
In slap of sea-water.
Men come, kneel,
Kiss the young hair
Of her thighs.
The sun glows, passes.
Night.
Slap of sea-water
Hurts, hurts.

RAPIST'S DAYDREAM

Stab
Your fingers
In beach sand
Smear
Your breasts, thighs
'Till bleeds
Drag
Your nakedness
(Sun now rises,
Glorious light awakens the sea)
Pull, though buttocks, breasts
Hurt–

I loved you, sweet.
You were the light of my day.
Now there is only
Sun, sea,
You
Washed up months later
Like pale fishbait.

TIGHTROPE WALKER

Desire strung tight.
The tightrope walker had crossed
Niagara, the Grand Canyon,
Stepped gingerly from tower to tower
With New York applauding from the grey deeps,
Grown ambitious,
Stretched rope from Mont Blanc
To the Matterhorn,
Defeated the winds and crossed.

Now what to do?
Chasms weren't deep enough.
So he stretched rope from earth
To the moon,
Wore a space suit,
Crossed.

His temper grew
Even as earth applauded
Thunderously.

To Jupiter he walked.
This would not do.

On Pluto's waste
He sat, furious.

Finally he stretched rope
Across the light years
Began his walk,
Then jumped.
It felt good, ever so good:
A million years he would crash somewhere.

THE CRIPPLE

"And all flesh shall see it together."

The Messiah wanders rooms
Of an oriental home.
Defeatist quiet of night.
A dog, crippled,
Whines interruption
From the bush,
Whine dies gracelessly
'Cross risen glory
Of choral crescendo
Leaving the windows,
Entering still brush,
Far in the night
Heard,
Whine of a cripple
Bent low to black earth,
Singing:
"And all flesh. . ."

SILVER FISH
(as told a psychiatrist)

I was far out at sea then,
Sailing my dinghy to Siberia.
The weather'd been rough,
And then another time so calm
I had to row, row, row
My boat, and the ocean
Is very big, I felt small,
Sailing to Siberia.
It was night when it happened,
And raining: in the blackness of sea
Suddenly I saw a big silver fish
Swimming beside my boat,
And smiling the funniest smile
You ever saw.
It shined so, I reached out
To touch it.
But it backed away.
I leaned further, the fish swam off,
And I plunged headlong in the sea.
The boat blew away, rain kept falling,
And it was all black water, black was the color
And I was drowning.
Then suddenly the silver fish was under me,
I was holding it around the neck
And it was carrying me, far across the sea.
Early in the morning it left me on the beach,
Not far from where I had started. Smiling
It swam away, and was gone.

Doctor, it makes me believe in *fate*.
You know, *destiny*.
A purpose, somehow.
I was sailing my dinghy to Siberia,
And this fish. . .

HAREM

Moods stretch themselves at my feet,
Yawn,
Sleep, waiting for me to choose.
Which one today?

For John Sole:

FABRICATION YARD BLUES

Dusk. Young man
Wandering among pipes.
It will rain tonight,
Sea clouds broadcast
The truth: it will rain.
Wind kicks up his hair,
He stares.
Casuarina trees whisper back and forth,
Like old scholars
Beyond the fuel tanks,
Murmur truth.
Big ships in solemn rows
Lie miles out–have entered
The eternal scheme of things
Anchored, still.
The big cranes, necks bowed,
Submissive. He turns.
Whispers, wind,
Hints all around:
Yes, it will rain tonight,
And tomorrow will be
And, yes. . .

TO–

In deep
Of night wind sails
A gleam–
In funnel
Of moonlight,
Where the senses
Meet–joined in awe
Of a whale
Wandering to–
To–

(Intellect,
Silenced once more
To know all paths
Circle
The dumb)

RADIO

Saxophone blues
Wax in the rain.
It's spilling from sea
This Sunday, pools reflect
Melancholy thoughts,
Fluttering palms
Appear tired of it all.
Saxophone plays,
Pumping some player's
Blue mood into rain, wind,
The grey indifference of it
Pounding, pounding
Wearing us
Washing us
Away, pumping
Something of some
Sad mood felt once
And soon to be washed away.

LECTURE

"Basically, sir,
It's a problem of filling
A vast space.
With what, of course,
Is the real question.
Morning comes,
It always does;
The day follows.
Well, then what?
Night. You see,
The trees always bend in the wind,
Babies are always born somewhere,
Dogs bark. It's basic.
The sea, Eternal Mother
Of poets, just eats up
And regurgitates all things,
The great pump driving all pattern.
The world is very full–
And I confess, sir,
I love to watch dogs run–
But the food doesn't satisfy.
Space is hungry, though fat to bursting.
It's a problem, sir,
Of filling *that* space."

ATTEMPTED RESCUE

"Help!" was the call.

Hm. But from where?

I glanced 'round.

Nothing around the typewriter
Or beyond the pipe rack.
My pen lay unconcerned
As usual. Desk solid.

The rug. Nothing there
Or under the desk.

Window. Outside
Sea beat rocks, sand boiled,
Usual. Certainly nothing there.

I even opened my Nietzsche,
But Zarathustra was asleep.

I began to worry.

Flung aside books.
Ripped out files.
Flicked off pictures. Nothing on the wall.
Ripped, frantic.

"Help!" frantic.

"SHINE A LIGHT ON ME"

Black rooms–
TV tubes shine.
Dark heads
In the shadows:
Shine a light on them.

I knew a family,
Daughter was sweet
Mother a good woman
Father a hard working man.
Came to visit one evening
Entered the black room:
Three heads bent on the light
That shines, and little children
Running about, in and out of the light
Silent–not a sound from them.
Though in the contemporary mode
Their worship proved to be lengthy.
With all due respect
I finally departed. Outside–
Stars, those many suns
Remote, cold
I bent, silent.
Nearly on my knees, oh Lord.

IT MAY BE ONLY IN SHADOWS

It may be only in shadows
Dreams roost, fancies fly
Only in darkness,
Delight is deep
Only where passionate to be love
We crack in fragments
Our world
Split and unholy

We will root a garden
A thousand manifold
When we break
And cry,
Seed will be
Our hopes and tears,
Our wanting and withdrawal
Like patter of light rain
On leaves: wet and life,
And melancholy sometimes

Sometimes a flower
In the darkness awaiting dawn
A single flower

SISTER

Past:

The round sun squanders
Its light on the land.
The river runs lazily by.
From the trees
Her round smile squanders
Her love on the land
Her laughter kips to the sky.

Present:

Sadness curled in the bosom of
  spring
Must await the older year
To wing, like the blackbird,
Toward the lonely sunset
Of age. She is older,
Pensive the shade of her face
More often now,
The eye grown more keen,
The heart of youth
Restrained.

ON READING A FEW CONTEMPORARY POEMS

It's a despair–
Drunk with the power of his own
He builds of sticks
And bare, worn cloth
His home,
Jars the visitor
With tangled outcries
Of crippled walls,
Bellows down the stairwell
(The steps fell through yesterday)
"Come visit my boudoir!"
Pouting all the while
The swollen, sagging
Sadness of walls

And mirrors too
Replying a distorted shape
On the poor human who
Tried merely to visit
This poet
And admire him.

PALM

Palm
Craving
Cry of the ravished soul
For milk of body's calm
And full

Nursing from fire-bitten deep
The sacrifice:
The want
Coursing tall straight

As palm
Craving

Maddening
Rapacious
For milk
For moon
For monstrous copulation

Pounding
Sucking him
Craving him–
Till palm
Crashes to sea,
Root cut and rent and
Roaring discontent:

By water's easy charm
Devoured,
And milk-dried,
Murdered.

APPEAL

In white of your sheets
Body white
The dry bone sun
Bleaching your walls
All colorless

(Vision dies with the sun)

In the wet of your loins' jungle
I lay my head, my dear
Aware
Only
Of the sweat
Of our flesh
The mutual annointment
Of our dreams

Grown white
Chaste
Colorless

Diminished
I could curl in your big hairs
Cling like the jungle baby
To its mama
Appeal to the fleshiness of your sex
For shelter
Diminished

When passion to penis
The long hungry stick
Of the blind
Bent man
Stumbles, now slightly mad,
For shelter

And would feast upon your eyes
With my bleached eyes
For the bone sun
Troubles your soul not,
Your big nipples
Your big belly not,
And your sweat gleams in the sun
Like a joyous chorus

So you laugh
So curl me to you
So keep me to you

A man wasted his eyes on the sun
In night alleys he sucked his wants;
Eyes chastened and white
His hands, like the jungle baby's,
Groped

So you laugh
So keep me to you

TOWARD BIRTH

The mind blew
Squally the rage
The remorse
For ruined with drink
It blew itself out last night

And set to wandering
The night long
Looking to fill the gap

Left when all its little power
Scattered the pieces
The furniture
Long accustomed
And glass
Too fragile
Smashed
The niceness
And entered the mud
The night long
Looking to quell
The quiet horror
Of who I was no more

You
Who let me touch
Round maiden, you

Will you save me?
Make me your roundness of vision
And feel?

You see,
Thought won't put it right
Won't justify
It
That I was

Like you I should be born
Wise
Because round–
And unquestioned
Round maiden, you

Draw me from the night
To watch with round eyes
Unsullied world
Shaped round
Unthought
Perfect

No longer the mind's scheme
The mean little tricks
Creative little tricks
Smart
But smashed, this night–

Mere furniture bits

Babbling in mud

Broken, maiden,

Wanting only eyes

That feel, shape

Round wonder of world

And voice that cries

Sheer pleasure

Of your giving me

REFLECTION

The wild birds of fall
Lift easily their wings
And are gone. The marshes grow cold.
Nude trees along the hills
Pierce the cold in knifeform,
Yet in the pale light of this evening
Easily be the things they are
Embrace the austere night
Without question.

Will the moon sing
Or simply stare?
The cold limbs of the wood
Add hush to the wind
Accept moonlight on their flesh
Like a baby taken to breast;

For the cold, love, hurts only a poet's soul.

The grass crackles—ice has arrived
Gripped the ground and the waiting seed,
Reached a cold hand to the roots;
All is stilled into the grace of seasonal things
That unthinking easily follow to their fulfillment
The ordained.

We will live and die, love,

But will we be graced as these?

Nietzsche cried, "*Fliege fort*! *Fliege fort*!"

The autumn hurt his eager soul,
Eager for life, to bud and grow
A mighty tree of dominance on the land
And rescue from the ordinary
The course of things, he hurt
At sight of this. He loved too much.

To defy? Shall we defy?
Cry fruitfulness our freedom
Then run, run, run when no longer the leaves bud
And all has turned to still?
Or when autumn closes our souls
Will we remain entwined
Like moonlight to the branch
To await our next spring?
In the autumn twilight
Easily lift our wings
Without thought of loss,
Be gone to our south
Accepting?

Will we yet love, my dear,
Because we did not love too much?

BABBLE OR,

Jejune

Juni

Juni

Juni

Jejune

Jap

Jop

Jeep

Jejune

Jack

Jock

Jeeeeeck

Ock!

Jejune, my dear

I am hungry

I am hungry

PLEASE

FEED

ME

NOSTALGIA

Snow
And the gloom of the overcast
Afternoon
On a hillside
Looking
Into it
Seeing
Gloom of long heartache
Snowing now
Snowing
Bringing white, calm
To an old, worn hillside
Of a life.

CHANT

I will climb the mountain
I will cross the sea
I will kiss the wind's
Loose flowing, be

Wild, a tumult
All gracious
Me

Storm the spaces
Crack the joints
Of old man earth, then
Laugh those joints to health
And wealth

Weep blessings, on the sky cry,
Shriek horrors in the caves,
Rave at times, rave

I will be
The rock of the desert
When you pass by,
See the infinite blues
When you cry, deep in the tissue
Of things we need,

See the infinite blues

I will bring you the sun
To shine, I will carry you,
Upon winds and whims and wants
Whirl with you in dance

In dance   In dance   In dance

I will die
Only
Wrapped round with you–

Be buried, as dust in the eye
Of old man earth, when he wept,
Cleansed it clean to the ground,
And laughed at the brief nuisance
Of my pain

CPSIA information can be obtained
at www.ICGtesting.com
Printed in the USA
LVOW08s1324181217
560164LV00002B/238/P